# PHYSICS FOR CLASS 9

## SIDE BOOK FOR PHYSICS CLASS 9



ADITYA RAJ ANAND

## TABLE OF CONTENTS

---------------------- Team Science laws -----------------------

# Contents

# Foreword

About Author

Hello, My name is Aditya Raj Anand an author, digital marketer, blogger, and an entrepreneur. My entrepreneur journey started from 2018 when I completed my schooling. Currently I am doing my bachelor of science in mathematics, after that I have decided to do my Master's in Physics, which I love to demonstrate.

How i become a digital marketing and web development.

As I told you when I completed my schooling from CBSE, my financial condition was not so good to carry forward my dreams. My dreams was to go in IITs. But unfortunately it was a complete disaster for me to change my path.

But the attachment to the science has not gone by me. So, i decided to start my first blog on science i.e, sciencelaws.in, here I started my passion to demonstrating science in easy language that an Evey student can understand and feel physics, chemistry.

When I was studying, I also feel the problems to understand science. Because science can be understood if it is expressed in easy language.

So, i decided language will not make the problem to understand science for anyone more.

So, I started writing, this book take me a 3 years of publishing. Aslo it was my childhood dream even before the dream of IIT.

# 1

# UNIT AND MEASUREMENT

**Unit of Measurement and time**

**Physics**:- The study of nature and natural things.

- **It is the made of greek word " Fusis" means natural things and nature.**
- It means that physics is the study of nature and its laws.
- Physics is the foundation of engineering and technology.
- Physics is based in experiment when experiments are done then it measure with the help of physical quantity.
- Quantity means it represents the number.

**Physical quantity:**- It is represent of the physical laws in the term id quantity.

- It is of two types
- Scalar quantity and vector quantity.
- Scalar quantity means it has only magnitude not direction.
- vector quantity means it has both magnitude and as well as direction.

**Units**

**It** is of two types

- Fundamental unit
- Derived unit

1. **Fundamental unit:-** It is not depend another unit, three fundamental unit are mass, length and Time.
2. **Derived unit:-** It is depend in fundamental unit.

**system of unit are four types**

1. **Mks system:-** In this system Length, Mass and Time are expressed in meter, Kilogram, and Second.
2. **Fps system:-** In this system Length, Mass and Time is expressed in Foot, Pound, second.
3. **CGs system:-** In this system Length, Mass and Time is expressed in Centimeter, Gram, second.
4. **S.I system;-** ( international System of Unit ) In S.I system having seven fundamental unit.

**30 physical quantities with their si units and cgs units**

Here is a collection of 30 fundamental and derived physical quantities which commonly used in physics with their si units and CGS units. Also describe the derived quantity with derivation.

We have already discussed about the definition of physical quantity in the above definition. But lets define the physical quantity in another words.

**Physical quantity are those quantities which represents the quantities of any material with the help of some symbols attached with numerical values.** For example a container contains 6 kilograms of wheat. So we can write 6 kg. Here kg is the physical quantity attached with numerical value of 6.

As we have already seen above that, **Physical quantities are two types first is fundamental quantity and second is derived quantity**. These are the following 30 physical quantities (both fundamental and derived) with their si units and CGS units. Before we start discussing following 30 physical quantities. Please note that some quantities are derived from fundamental quantity.

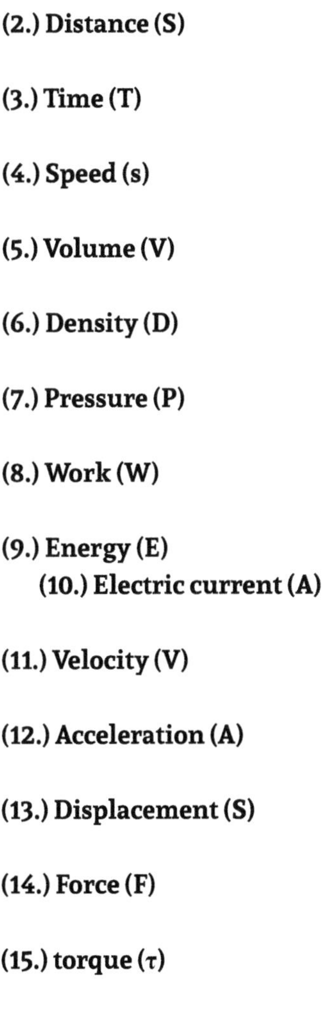

**30 physical quantities with their si units and cgs units**

**(1.) Mass (M)**

**(2.) Distance (S)**

**(3.) Time (T)**

**(4.) Speed (s)**

**(5.) Volume (V)**

**(6.) Density (D)**

**(7.) Pressure (P)**

**(8.) Work (W)**

**(9.) Energy (E)**

**(10.) Electric current (A)**

**(11.) Velocity (V)**

**(12.) Acceleration (A)**

**(13.) Displacement (S)**

**(14.) Force (F)**

**(15.) torque (τ)**

**(16.) Electric field (E)**

**(17.) Angular velocity (ω)**

**(18.) Linear momentum (P)**

**(19.) Magnetic dipole moment (?)**

**(20.) Thrust (T)**

**(21.) Temperature (T)**

**(22.) Frequency (μ)**

**(23.) Amount of substance (Mol)**

**(24.) Concentration (C)**

**(25.) Power (P)**

**(26.) Impulse (I)**

**(27.) Angle (∠)**

**(28.) Weight (W)**

**(29.) Magnetic field (B)**

**(30.) Gravitation (G)**

Lets discuss all of these physical quantities with their definition along with their si and cgs unit.

**(1.) Mass (M)**

Mass is the scale of measurement of inertia of any body or matter. mass represent the quantity that a body have. greater the mass of a body, less in impact of force in it. mass do not depends on shape and size of a body. that means the greater size of a body need not have a greater mass or vice-versa.

- S.I unit of mass:- Kilogram (Kg)
- CGS unit of mass:- Gram (g)

**(2.) Distance (S)**

The actual path covered by the body during the whole journey. It is denoted by S. distance is different from displacement. both have some differences between them. Distance may be in straight line, curved line, or zigzag line. Distance can never be zero untill or unless the body is at rest.

- S.I unit of distance:- Meter (m)
- CGS unit of distance:- Centimetre (cm)

**(3.) Time (T)**

Time is an illusion that loses in every second. time is an infinite unfinished continuous events that exist in present, fall in past and will next in future. time is denoted by t.

- S.I unit of time:- Second (s)
- CGS unit of time:- second (s)

**(4.) Speed (s)**

Speed is define as the total distance travelled by the body to the total time taken. In other words speed is determined by the distance covered in a specific time period by the body. It is denoted by s.

- S.I unit of speed:- meter / sec (m/s)
- CGS unit of speed:- centimetre / sec (cm/s)

**(5.) Volume (V)**

The maximum dimensional area covered by an object in length, breath and height. It is denoted by V. volume is affected by shape and size of a body. means if the body has greater shape and size it may be the body has larger volume or vice-versa.

- S.I unit of volume:- meter cube (m3)
- CGS unit of volume:- centimetre cube (cm3)

**(6.) Density (D)**

Density is define as the mass of a body per unit volume. That means if a body has volume 'v' and mass 'm' then density is equal to m/v.

- S.I unit density:- kilogram / m2 (kg/m3)
- CGS unit density:- gram / cm3 (g /cm3)

**(7.) Pressure (P)**

Pressure is the force exerted in a unit area of an object. It is denoted by P. pressure is also define as the force per unit area. given by P = F / A.

- S.I unit of pressure:- Newton / m2 (N / m2) or Pascal
- CGS unit pressure:- Dyne / cm2

**(8.) Work (W)**

In physics, If a force is applied on a body and the body get displaces from its initial position and covers some distance then work is done. It is denoted by W. work can also be described as the dot product of force and displacement. given by W = F.s.

- S.I unit of work:- Joule (N-m) or Newton-meter.
- CGS unit of work:- Erg (dyne-cm) or Dyne-centimetre

**(9.) Energy (E)**

The ability to do some work is called energy. energy can neither be created nor be destroyed but it can be converted into one form to another form. like electric energy into light energy. It is denoted by E.

- S.I unit of energy:- Joule
- CGS unit of energy:- Erg

**(10.) Electric current (A)**

It is the flow of electron from one potential to another potential. Flow of electron create potential difference between two points so that electricity generated. It is denoted by A.

- S.I unit of electric current:- Ampere
- CGS unit of electric current:- Biot

**(11.) Velocity (V)**

Velocity is define as the distance travelled by the body per unit time in a given direction. Velocity is vector quantity. because it has both magnitude and direction. It is denoted by V. velocity can also be described as the displacement per unit time.

**Velocity = Displacement / time**

- S.I unit of velocity:- meter / sec. (m /s)
- CGS unit of velocity:- centimetre / sec. (cm /s)

**(12.) Acceleration (A)**

Acceleration is the change in velocity with respect to time. In other words, it is the final displacement minus initial displacement whole divided by time. It is denoted by A. Acceleration is vector quantity.

- S.I unit of acceleration:- meter / sec2 (m / s2)
- CGS unit of acceleration:- centimetre / sec2 (cm / s2)

**(13.) Displacement (S)**

It is the shortest distance covered by the body in whole journey. In other words, displacement is equal to the distance between initial position and final position of a body. It is denoted by S. Distance may be zero.

- S.I unit of displacement:- meter (m)
- CGS unit of displacement:- centimetre (cm)

**(14.) Force (F)**

Force is define as the push or pull of an object is called force. In other words, force is the product of mass and acceleration. It is denoted by F. where F = ma.

- S.I unit of force:- Newton (Kg. m /s2)
- CGS unit of force:- Dyne (g. cm /s2)

**(15.) torque (τ)**

It is the measurement of the force acting on a body to determine how much it cause to rotate the body. It is denoted by τ. It is vector quantity.

- S.I unit of torque:- Newton-meter (N-m)
- CGS unit of torque:- Dyne-centimetre

**(16.) Electric field (E)**

It is a reason where electric current can be experienced. In other words, electric field is the area where the electric field lines exist. It is denoted by E.

- S.I unit of electric field:- Newton / coulomb (volt / meter)
- CGS unit of electric field:- Dyne / biot-sec.

**(17.) Angular velocity (ω)**

Rate of change of angular displacement with respect to time. On other hand angular velocity is how fast the body is moving with respect to time.

- S.I unit of angular velocity:- radian / sec
- CGS unit of angular velocity:- per second

**(18.) Linear momentum (P)**

Linear momentum is defined as the product of mass and velocity. It is denoted by P. yhe formula of linear momentum is P = mv. It is vector quantity.

- S.I unit of liner momentum:- Kg. m /s
- CGS unit of linear momentum:- g. cm /s

**(19.) Magnetic dipole moment (?)**

Magnetic dipole moment represent the magnetic strength of the magnet with the help of quantity. It is denoted by ?. It is vector quantity because it has both magnitude and direction.

- S.I unit of magnetic dipole moment:- weber-meter
- CGS unit of magnetic dipole moment:- emu. erg/G

**(20.) Thrust (T)**

Thrust is the types of force act on upward direction in water.

- S.I unit of thrust:- Newton
- CGS unit of thrust:- Dyne

**(21.) Temperature (T)**

It is define as the how hotness and coldness of the body is. It is denoted by T. In other words temperature indicates that how hot or cold a body is.

- S.I unit of temperature:- kelvin (k)
- CGS unit of temperature:- kelvin

**(22.) Frequency (μ)**

It is number of cycle of a wave passing in one second. In other words it is cycle per second.

- S.I unit of frequency:- Hertz (Hz)

- CGS unit of frequency:- Hertz

**(23.) Amount of substance (Mol)**

Amount of substance is defined as the total number of soute present in total number of solvent.

- S.I unit of amount of substance:- Mole
- CGS unit of amount of substance:- mole

**(24.) Concentration (C)**

Concentration is define as the total number of solute or solvent present in a unit volume of solution. In other words it calculate the mass of solute or solvent per unit volume. It is denoted by C.

- S.I unit of concentration:- kilogram / m3
- CGS unit of concentration:- gram / cm3

**(25.) Power (P)**

The rate of doing work is called power. power is work per unit time. It is denoted by P.

- S.I unit of power:- joule / sec (watt)
- CGS unit of power:- erg / sec

**(26.) Impulse (I)**

Impulse is the force acting for a short period of time.

- S.I unit of Impulse:- Newton-second
- CGS unit of Impulse:- Dyne-second

**(27.) Angle (∠)**

It is unitless that expressed in terms of theta.

**(28.) Weight (W)**

Weight is the force acting in downward direction to the center of the earth. It is the downward force.

- S.I unit of weight:- Newton
- CGS unit of weight:- Dyne

**(29.) Magnetic field (B)**

It is the reason where magnetic force is experienced. It is denoted by B.

- S.I unit:- Tesla
- CGS unit:- oersted

**(30.) Gravitation (G)**

It the pulling force acting in downward direction toward the center of the planet.

- S.I unit:- Newton / kg
- CGS unit:- Dyne / g

here you find the actual meaning of scalar and vector quantity. If we define scalar and vector quantity in simple word we can say that scalar quantity are those which have only magnitude not direction, but vector quantity are those which have both magnitude as well as direction. difference between scalar and vector quantity are given below the page for better understanding of these quantities.

There are many topics covered in this articles like,

1. **What is scalar and vector quantity?**
2. **List of scalar and vector quantities and their units.**
3. **Difference between scalar and vector quantity.**
4. **Product of scalar and vector quantity.**
5. **What is scalar and vector field?**
6. **20 examples of scalar and vector quantity.**
7. **characteristics of scalar and vector quantities.**
8. **Types of vector.**
9. **vector addition and subtraction.**
10. What is scalar and vector quantity?

## *What is scalar and vector quantity?*

**scalar quantity:-** Those quantity which has only magnitude not direction are called scalar quantity.

for example length, mass, speed, work, density, volume etc.

lets understand by taking examples If we say the body have 10 kg of mass it doesn't means not 10 kg of mass in north or south direction.

In other words Those quantity which has only one dimension described by single element like one constant and one variable. for example 5m, 6cm, 2kg, 4mm etc.

**Vector quantity:-** Those quantity which has both magnitude and a specific direction are called vector quantity.

for example Displacement, Force, acceleration, velocity, torque, momentum etc.

lets understand by taking examples, suppose 2N of force act on the body in North direction, A body is accelerating 5m/s2 in upward direction, Weight (W= mg) of a body acted in the downward direction.

In other word Those quantity which has both two dimension and three dimension described by some more elements like 5m North, 3m/s2, 6m/s, 5N, etc.

## ***List of scalar and vector quantities and their units.***

scalar quantity
unit of scalar quantity
vector quantity
unit of vector quantity
Mass
kilogram(kg)
Displacement
meter(m)
Distance

Meter(m)
Velocity
m/s
Time
Second(s)
Acceleration
m/s2
Speed
m/s
Force
Newton(N)
Volume
m3
Torque
Newton meter(N-m)
Density
kg/m3
Electric field
volt per meter(v/m)
Pressure
Newton(N)
Angular velocity
radians per second
Work
Joule(J)
Linear momentum
kilogram meters per second(kg m/s)
Energy
Joule(J)
Magnetic dipole moment
Ampere meter(A-m)
Electric current
Ampere(A)
Thrust
Force(F)

## *20 examples of scalar and vector quantity.*

### 20 examples of scalar quantities

1. Mass
2. Distance
3. Time
4. Speed
5. Volume
6. Density
7. Pressure
8. Work
9. Energy
10. Electric Current
11. Length
12. Refractive Index
13. Area
14. Power
15. Heat
16. Temperature
17. Size
18. Calories
19. Frequency
20. Cost

### 20 examples of vector quantities

1. Displacement
2. Velocity
3. Torque
4. Thrust
5. Force
6. Acceleration
7. Electric field

8. Angular momentum
9. Angular velocity
10. Drift velocity
11. Magnetic dipole moment
12. Linear momentum
13. Average velocity
14. Magnetic field
15. Weight
16. Gravitational force
17. vector potential
18. Poynting vector
19. current density
20. Magnetisation

## *Difference between scalar and vector quantity.*

These are some differential points on scalars and vectors.

**Scalar quantity:-**

- Scalar quantity has only magnitude.
- They change if their magnitude change.
- They can be added according to ordinary laws of algebra.

**Vector quantity:-**

- vectors have both magnitude and direction
- They change if either their magnitude, direction or both change.
- They can be added only by using special laws of vector addition.

## *Product of scalar and vector quantity*

Scalar product and vector product are the two different ways of multiplying two vectors. Multiplication of scalar product has its own rule and Multiplication of vectors product has its own way.

**Scalar product (or dot product) of two vectors:-** The scalar or dot product of two vectors A and B is defined as the product of the magnitudes of vectors A and B and cosine of the angle θ between them.

**vector product (or cross product) of two vectors:-** The vector or cross product of two vectors is defined as the vector whose magnitude is equal to the product of the magnitudes of two vectors and sine of the angle between them and whose direction is perpendicular to the plane of the two vectors.

## *What is scalar and vector field?*

A scalar field is something that has a particular value at every point in space. for example temperature at every point on the earth has a particular value but if we move to and fro from that point then the value of temperature will change.

A vector field is just similar to scalar field because vector field also having a value at every point on space. but it has a value and direction at every point in space.

## *characteristics of scalar and vector quantities.*

Before knowing the characteristic of scalar and vector quantities. we have to know he meaning of characteristic.

characteristic means a quality of something that makes him/her/it different from other people or thing.

so here characteristic of scalar and vector quantity has little same that is magnitude. lets understand it in more detailed.

**characteristic of scalar quantities:-** scalar quantity has only magnitude. there is no need of direction. speed, distance, time, temperature these all do not need direction.

for example Ramesh played for 3 hours. here we do not need direction.

**characteristic of vector quantities:-** vector quantities has also magnitude but it needs direction for their illustration. displacement, velocity, acceleration, force etc acquires direction.

for example a body start moving by 3m/s in forward direction. here direction included for better illustration.

## *Types of vector.*

**Position vector:-** A vector which gives position of an object with reference to the origin of a co-ordinate system is called position vector.

**Displacement vector:-** It is that vector which tells how much and in which direction and object has changed its position in a given time interval.

**Polar vector:-** The vector which has a starting point or a point of application are called polar vector.

**Axial vector:-** The vector which represent rotational effect and act along the axis of rotation in right hand screw rule are called axial vector.

**Equal vector:-** Two vectors are said to be equal if they have the same magnitude and same direction.

**Negative of a vector:-** The negative of a vector is defined as another vector having the same magnitude but having an opposite direction.

**Modulus of vector:-** The modulus of a vector means the length or the magnitude of that vector.

**Unit vector:-** A unit vector is a vector of unit magnitude drawn in the direction of a given vector.

**Fixed vector:-** The vector whose initial point is fixed is called a fixed vector.

**Zero vector:-** a zero vector or null vector is a vector that has zero magnitude and an unknown direction.

## *vector addition and subtraction.*

Two vectors can be added or can be subtracted by their rules and laws. vectors can be added by two famous laws

- **Triangle law of vector addition:-** If two vectors can be represented both in magnitude and direction by the two sides of triangle taken in the same order, then their resultant is represented completely, both in magnitude and direction, by the third side of the triangle taken in the opposite order.

- **Parallelogram law of vector addition:-** If two vectors can be represented both in magnitude and direction by the two adjacent sides of a parallelogram drawn from a common point, then their resultant is completely represented, both in magnitude and direction, by the diagonal of the parallelogram passing through the point. see the above picture for more illustration.

Please note that the same rules and theory also use in subtraction of two vectors but you have to replace plus sign from the minus sign.

**FAQ on scalar and vector quantities**

**What is scalar and vector quantities?**

scalar quantities are those quantities which has only magnitude not direction. speed, time, distance etc.

vector quantities are those quantities which has both magnitude and a specific direction. displacement, velocity, acceleration etc.

**Is work scalar or vector?**

work is scalar quantity which has only magnitude. w= f.s work is dot product of force and displacement. and we know that dot product is scalar quantity.

**can a scalar be negative?**

Yes scalar can be negative. but it depends on situation and types of quantities. like temperature can be negative which is a scalar quantity.

**Is force a scalar quantity?**

No force is a vector quantity. because it has cross product of mass and acceleration. F= m✖?a cosθ.

**Where do we use vectors?**

vectors can be used in physics to represent physical quantities with direction in the upper head by arrow sign. it is used to represent displacement, velocity, acceleration, etc.

**Can you square a vector?**

No we cannot square a vector because a vector has both magnitude and direction. we can square its magnitude but not direction.

-------------- Team Science laws --------------

# 2

# Motion

## Motion

- In physics a things which can see, touch and feel is called object or body.
- It is the branch of physics which deals with the study of the object at rest and in motion.

## *Object in rest*

A body is said to be rest if it does not change its position with respect to its surrounding with the passage of time.

## *Object in motion*

If the position of the body changes its state with respect to its surrounding then body is called in motion.

### *Rest and motion are relative terms*

Rest and motion are relative terms because object can be at rest with respect to one things and in motion with respect to some other things at the same time, so motion is not absolute, it is relative. for example---

- Suppose you are sitting in a train which is moving then we are at rest with respect to the other passenger sitting in that compartment but in motion with respect to the objects on the ground.
- Our house is at rest with respect to the other house on the earth but it is in motion with respect to an observer on the moon.

## ***Types of motion***

One dimension, two dimension motion, three dimension motion.

**One dimension motion:-**

- **The** motion in a straight lines is called one - dimension motion.
- Moving of bus in a straight line.
- Falling of an apple from tree.
- If only co - ordinate is used from three co - ordinate x, y and z then the motion is one dimension motion.

**Two dimension motion;-**

- Motion in a plane is called two dimension motion.
- If only two co - ordinate is used from three co - ordinate x, y and z then it is called two dimension.
- The motion of object in horizontal and vertical circle.
- The earth revolving around the sun.
- S carom coin in motion.

**Three dimension motion;-**

- Motion in space is called three dimension motion.

- If all co - ordinate is used then it is called three dimension motion.

**Position:-**

- If particles on the origin then its position will be zero.
- If particles move along the positive direction of x - axis then its position positive.
- If particles moves in the negative direction of x – axis then the position is negative.

**Distance:-** The actual length of the path covered by an object is called distance.

- The length of the actual path between the initial and final position of the body is called the distance.
- Distance has no sense of direction hence distance is a scalar quantity.
- It's S.I unit is 'm' .
- Distance can never be negative.

**Displacement:-**

- The shortest distance between two points is called displacement.
- If the body moves in any direction then displacement is change in position.
- If the initial and final position of the body are same then the displacement will be Zero.
- Hence, from above result we can say that displacement will be positive, Negative or zero.
- Displacement has sense of direction therefore displacement is a vector quantity.
- S.I unit of displacement is 'm' .
- It is not depend on path but distance is depend on path.
- Distance is equal to displacement when it goes to straight line.

- If we move on the straight lines in positive direction then distance is equal to the displacement but we move in curved path then distance is greater than displacement.

## *Uniform and non uniform motion*

**Uniform motion:-** When a body moves in such a way that it covers equal distance in equal interval of time however small the time interval may be then speed is said to be uniform motion.

**Non uniform motion:-** if body travels equal distance in unequal interval of time/ unequal distance cover in equal interval of time then it is called non uniform motion.

## *What is Speed?*

- The distance traveled by a body per unit time over a short interval of time is called its speed.
- S.I unit of speed is m/s.
- C.Gs unit of speed is cm/s.
- speed is the scalar quantity.

## *What is Velocity?*

- The displacement covered by a body per unit time is called velocity.
- S.I unit of velocity is m/s.
- C.Gs unit is cm/s.
- velocity is vector quantity it has both magnitude and direction.

## *What is Average speed?*

- It is the ratio of total distance traveled by total time taken.
- It is a scalar quantity.
- It's S.I unit is m/s.
- It is denoted by 'V' .

## *Wha is Acceleration?*

Rate of change of velocity with respect to time.

Acceleration = final velocity - initial velocity/ time

a = v - u / t

- S.I unit of acceleration is m/s2.
- Acceleration may be positive, Negative or Zero.

## ***Acceleration are two types***

1. **Uniform Acceleration:-**

When a body travels in a straight lines and its velocity changes by equal amounts is equal interval of time then it is called Uniform acceleration.

2. **Non uniform Acceleration:-**

When the velocity of a body changes by unequal amount in equal interval of time then it is called non uniform acceleration.

- Positive acceleration is simply called acceleration.
- Negative acceleration is simply called Retardation.

**Three equation of motion**

1. First equation of motion

$$V = u + at$$

Proof :- we know that
acceleration = change in velocity/ time taken

$$a = v - u/t$$
$$at = v - u$$
$$at + u = v$$
or
$$v = u + at$$
Where,
V = final velocity
U = initial velocity
T = time
A = acceleration

2. Second equation of motion
S = ut + 1/2 at2
Proof

Average speed = u + v/2
Distance = Average speed * time
$$S =( u + v/2 )* t$$
We know that
$$v = u + at$$
put value of v
$$S = ut + ut + at2/ 2$$
$$= 2 ut + at\wedge 2/ 2$$
$$S = ut + 1/2 at2$$

3. Third equation of motion

v2 = u2 + 2as

We know that,
$$V = u + at$$

and ,

$$S = ut + 1/2\ at2$$

From $V = u + at$

$$t = v - u/a$$

$$S = ut + 1/2\ at2$$

$$S = u*( v -u/a) + 1/2 * a *( v -u/a )2$$

$$2as + u2 = v2$$

$$v2 = u2 + 2as$$

------------- Team Science laws --------------

# 3

# Force and Laws of Motion

**Force and Laws of Motion**

Force :- It may be defined as push or pull which produces (tends to produces) a change in the state of rest or uniform motion of a body or change in the direction of motion of the body.

i. Force may also change the Shape of the body or produces rotational effect.
v. Force is a vector quantity because Force have as well as magnitude and direction.
v. The non-living body also exert a Force.

**Example:**- (i) When we suspended a heavy block From a rope. The rope holds the block just as a man can hold in the air.

(ii) When a cork is dipped in Water it comes to the surface due to the upward. Force exerted by water.

**Galileo's Experiment: (Aristotle)**

(iii) When we comb our der hair and bring the comb close to bits of paper the piece jumps to the comb therefore, we can say the Force is interaction between two bodies.

i. A Greek philosopher give the idea that a constant Force is needed to keep a body moving with constant velocity it means that if a constant Force not applied the body will come to rest. Thus, the natural state of a body is that of rest.

In 17$^{th}$ century Galileo Galilei and Italian scientist opposed the idea of Aristotle according to Galileo no Force was needed to keep a body in constant velocity it means that natural state of a body it is oppose the change in its of motion.

**Newton's1$^{st}$ law of motion**

Every object continuous in a state of rest or of uniform motion in a straight line if external force no applied on the body.

'Inertia' this term is well known for those who take interest in physics. Inertia is a very important part of physics. But our question is from where this inertia came. So a quite simple answer would be from "Newton's laws of motion". So in this post we will not only discuss the types of inertia and their examples but also we will try to find out how inertia originated from Newton's law.

A famous person said that there are total 10% physics covered if you know Newton's laws. Here Newton's laws means not only three laws but all the portions including inertia, momentum, etc.

Now, let's focus on our main topic that is inertia of rest. So before we start the definition of Inertia. Let's understand what we have to know to understand full concept of inertia of rest.

**So these are the things and terms related to inertia that everyone should know to clear the full concept of inertia of rest.**

- What is inertia?
- Types of inertia?
- What is inertia of rest?
- Inertia of rest in terms of Newton's law.
- Deep discussion on inertia of rest.
- Property of inertia of rest.
- Factors depends on inertia of rest.
- One experiment to demonstrate inertia of rest.
- 8 most common examples of inertia of rest in our daily life.

## *What is inertia?*

We have studied in our previous classes that inertia is the tendency of a body to remain it in their original state. No matter whether the body is moving or stop.

In more simple way we can say that inertia is the legacy or identity of any object. Means that inertia indicates or tells about the nature of a body. But is that's it about inertia? Is there this limited information available about inertia?

We can't say anything because in our childhood we have just studied that much. So it's time to know more about inertia.

Apart from the types of inertia that we will discuss later in this post. Let's take a deep breath and lost on the deep analysis of inertia.

Everything in this universe is in two forms whether it may be in position of rest or in motion. Those bodies which are in a state of raised in this universe may because of some universal force or gravity. And those bodies which are in a state of motion may because of the some same universal force of gravity.

So how we can say that there has the body's tendency to remains at in state of rest or in state of motion. If something is in a state of rest may be because some force act on it. For example let's suppose a football is placed in playground. Now here two situation arises.

**Situation No 1 :-**

- The football on the ground is at in a state of rest may because no one applied an external force on it.

**Situation No 2 :-**

The football on the ground is at in state of rest may because of the flat surface with gravity pulling. If the ground will be incline it will start moving with gravity force.

No from the above discussion on two situation. We have understood that inertia of anybody it is not only sustainable with external force. But also unbalanced force.

Hence, in the definition of inertia we have to say that inertia is the tendency of a body to remains its state of rest or uniform motion until or unless no any external or unbalanced force applied on it.

**Let's understand the concept of unbalanced force in Inertia.**

As we have discussed above about two situation. The first is about no external force applied on the rest football. And the second is gravity. So here in this case of rest football on the ground. The gravitational force has cancelled by upward Normal force. Hence the resultant force will be zero. Therefore, the football has a tendency of rest called football has inertia.

## *Types of Inertia*

According to Newton's first law of motion. The inertia can be divided into three parts.

- Inertia of rest.
- Inertia of motion.
- Inertia of direction.

Today in this post we will only discuss about inertia of rest. Not only the definition but also the top 8 examples of inertia of rest that we have seen in our daily life.

All the scientific phenomenon whether it inertia, Newton's laws, thermodynamics laws, gravitation etc can be seen in our daily life style. We have to just open our scientific mind of seen.

As similar to other phenomenon that happen in our daily life. The one most common is inertia of rest. So before we discuss the examples of inertia of rest. Let's take an overview about what is inertia of rest?

## ***What is inertia of rest in simple words***

Inertia of rest is simply defined as the tendency of any body to remains the original state of rest is called Inertia of rest.

In other words, if a body is in position of rest means it is not moving from one place to another then we can say that the body has a tendency to remains in state of rest.

## *Inertia of rest in terms of Newton's law*

The concept of inertia of rest, inertia of motion and inertia of direction comes from Newton's first law of motion.

According to Newton's first law of motion those bodies which are in state of rest remains in rest or in motion remains in motion until or unless no external or unbalanced force applied on it.

The definition is quite similar to the definition of inertia because the concept of Newton's first law and inertia is same.

Inertia is originated from Newton's first law. You can also say that inertia is the refined concept of Newton's first law.

## ***Deep discussion on Inertia of rest***

Newton discovered three laws. Galileo was the first who talked about laws of motion and gravitation. But after the death of Galileo, it was Newton who published the three laws of motion called Newton's laws of motion. After the discovery of Newton's first law, the concept of inertia came.

Now, the question is why the concept of inertia came from Newton's first law. So the answer is hidden in the definition of Newton's first law.

As we know, Newton's first law says that any body which have a state of rest to remains in rest or which have a state of motion it also remains in motion. For example if a body is moving, it doesn't means some force is responsible for moving that body. It is the tendency of that body to keep moving forever until or unless no external or unbalanced force applied to it.

As we know the definition of inertia of rest is extracted from Newton's first law. Now, the meaning of inertia is also quite similar to the meaning of mass. That means if a body has some masses, then it has also some inertia.

So we can say that inertia is a type of force that can be experienced when the state of body changes. For example if we sit in a bus which is in rest. And if the bus suddenly start moving we will experience some backward force because of inertia of rest. Hence, we conclude that inertia is also a type of force.

## ***Property of inertia of rest***

These are some properties that describe the inertia of rest.

- The first property of inertia of rest of a body is that it resist the change in their state of motion.
- The second property of inertia of rest of a body is that some forces are necessary to apply to move the rest body.
- The last property is that when a body is at rest. It has a definite amount of inertia due to certain mass of the body.

## ***Factors depends on inertia of rest***

There are two simple factors that the inertia of rest of a body depends.

1. The first factors that affect Inertia of rest is mass of a body. Means more the masses of a body. More will be inertia and less will be mass the less will be inertia.
2. The second factors that affect Inertia of rest is density of a body. More will be density the higher will be inertia and vice versa.

## ***One experiment to demonstrate inertia of rest***

To perform this experiment take one glass, one square playing card and one 5 rupees coin.

Now, we have all the things that is necessary to perform the experiment of inertia of rest. We will perform this experiment in five simple steps. So let's start.

Step 1 :- Take one 5 rupees coin, one square size playing card and one glass.

Enter Caption

Step 2 :- Now, placed this card on the above of the glass filled with water.

Step 3 :- After placing the card, let's place teh coin above the card.

Enter Caption

Step 4 :- Pull the playing card suddenly in backward direction.

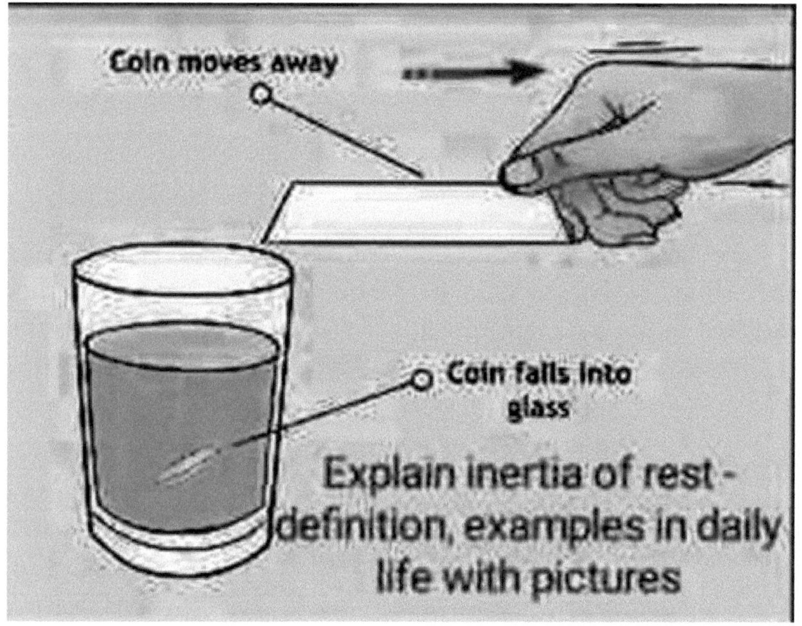


Enter Caption

Step 5 :- After pulling it in inward direction the coin falls down vertically in the glass. This is because the original state of the coin was at rest. But after suddenly pulling the card. The card Start moving in backward direction. But card has a tendency to remains its state of rest. So it falls down vertically. This shows that the coin follows the concept of inertia of rest.

## *8 most common examples of inertia of rest in our daily life.*

Here are the 8 examples of inertia of rest with explanation that we experiences in our day to day life.

1. **Felling jerk after bus start moving.**

This happens as follows, when we sat on a stop bus and if the bus start moving suddenly then we feel a background jerk in our body. This is due to the inertia of rest. Because the bus get motion but our body has the tendency to remains it in state of rest.

**2. Coin drop vertically when the card flick.**

Now, take a playing card, a coin and a glass of water. Put the card on the top of the glass and put coin on the card. Now, flick or pull the card in the backward direction. You will find that due to the suddenly pulling of the card, the coin drop into the glass filled with water.

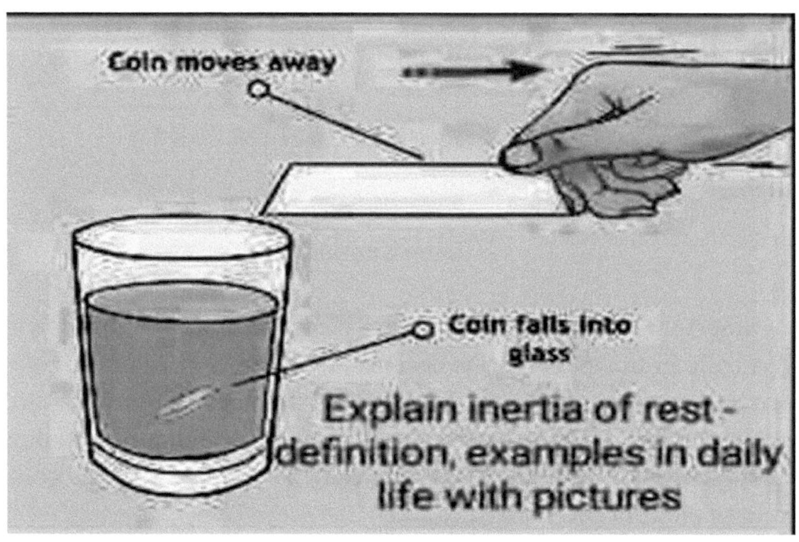


Enter Caption

This happen as follows When we put coin and card on the glass. All these things was in state of rest. But after the we have pulled the card, we applied a force only on the card not the coin placed above the card. So due to the tendency of the coin to remains in original state i.e, rest. The coin falls vertically into the glass.

**3. Dust appear after shaking of dirty clothes.**

You have must seen that when we beat the dirty clothes or blankets with sticks. Or even if we shake dirty clothes with our hands in sunlight. The dust particles appears to moving in surrounding of clothes. Have you ever be think, why this happens. So this happens because of inertia of rest of dust particles.

This happens as follows, when we start beating the dirty clothes. The the cloth start moving in to and fro motion but the dust particles remains in state of rest. So due to not moving of dust particles with cloth it seems like moving in surrounding.

**4. Bullet makes a fine hole in glass**

This example is very interesting. You have seen in many movies that when a person shoots a glass door with gun. The bullet of the gun makes a fine hole to the size of the bullet without breaking the glass.

This happens as follows : initially the glass of the window are in rest. But after the gun fired. The bullet strikes with the glass in a perticular are with respect to the size of the bullet. And dur to the very high speed of the bullet. The glass piece from that area where the bullet strikes goes with the bullet and makes a fine hole.

**5. Glass not falls after table cloth removed.**

Many magician performed this magic in different different show. You have must seen that magic.

Let's perform that magic. Take a glass of water. Placed it on the table with table cloth.

Now, pull the table clothes with high force. You will notice that the glass filled with water not drop. Even their water. So how this happens.

This happens as : when we suddenly pull the table clothes. The cloth get a motion and leave the tendency of rest. But the water glass was still in state of rest. Hence, due to the inertia of rest the glass not falls down after the cloth removed from the table.

**6. Falling of fruits after shaking tree.**

When we shake guava, or mango tree. The fruits fall down because the fruits wants to remains in state of rest.

**7. Moved backward when train start from station.**

When train start moving. The wheal of the train gets motion but the passenger has a tendency to remains in state of rest. Hence, it experienced a jerk in backward direction.

**8. Shutter feels heavy during shop close.**

If you noticed that when we pull the shutter to close the shop. The shutter feels quite heavy. This is due to the two reasons. First is due to their high mass and other is due to inertia of rest.

Before we apply a pulling force to the shop Shutter. The shutter is in state of rest. Even after applying force the shutter wants to remains at in state of rest. Hence, we feels heavy during shop close.

After a long discussion on Inertia of rest. The time has come to talk about inertia of motion. Not only the definition but also 10 examples of inertia of motion that we have all experienced in our day to day life.

But before we go further, let's make a table of contents for this post.

**Topic covered in this lecture**

- What is an Inertia of motion?
- Formula of inertia of motion.

Q. What is inertia give an example of inertia of motion also explain which of the following has more inertia an empty box or a box full of books?

- Daily life examples of inertia of motion with visual picture.
- Application of inertia of motion.
- Where is Inertia of motion came from?
- Why inertia of motion related to Newton's first law of motion?

All the above topic are well explained in the following notes. So let's start.

## *What is inertia of motion?*

If we talk about only inertia, neither rest nor motion. Then it is a tendency of a body to keep their original state.

So, Inertia of motion is defined as the tendency of a body to keep their original state of motion forever. Untill or unless an external force is applied to it.

Please note that :- In inertia of motion, the direction of the moving object also constant. Means will be moving in only one direction forever.

Let's take an example to understand the inertia of motion more clearly.

**Case 1:-**

Suppose a car is running on a straight road at a speed of 40 km/h. After 5 hours of constant moving, a curve turning has come. Now, if we didn't apply the external force (or brake) the car will be accident.

But if we apply the brake to the car, suddenly we feel a forward jerk. This jerk is because of inertia of motion.

This explains as follows : When we apply the brake the car has stopped but our body has a tendency to keep their original state of motion. Due to this we feel jerk in the forward direction.

**Case 2:-**

Suppose the same car is running on a straight road at a speed of 40 km/h. After 3 hours of constant moving a road breaker has come.

Now, when the car cross the breaker, the wheel of the car leave the ground for some minor second and after that it again touches the ground. But due to this we felt a jump inside the car.

This jump is because of inertia of motion. This explains as follows:

While the constant moving of the car. Our body is in state of rest with respect to other person inside the car. But in motion with respect to the people who has seen from outside the car.

Please note that :- This case is also a good example of rest and motion are relative terms.

So, after crossing the road breaker our body gain some motion but after some micro second it again touches the ground. So we felt jump in upward direction.

**Case 3:-**

Suppose, we are sitting in the same car. After some time, if we change the direction of the car. We felt down in the right side because of the inertia of direction.

## Rest and motion are relative terms.

Suppose a person is standing on the moon. We can say that person is in state of rest with respect to another person stand beside them. But in motion with respect to that person who seen both of them from earth.

Let's take another example to illustrate our above example.

Suppose we are sitting on a running train. Here we can say that we are in state of rest with respect to other passages sitting besides us. But we are still in motion with respect to the passages standing on the platform.

## *formula of inertia of motion*

Please note that there is no definite formula to calculate the inertia of motion, rest or direction.

Inertia is a phenomenon in science. It is not a mathematical concepts or equations.

The inertia of momentum has a formula. But not inertia of motion.

Inertia of motion is used to understand the concept of the questions. Inertia can be used to clean the concept of Newton's first law of motion.

## *Q. What is inertia give an example of inertia of motion also explain which of the following has more inertia an empty box or a box full of books?*

In most simple words, Inertia is the tendency or behaviour of a body that helps them to keep their original state unless or until an external force is applied to it.

Please not that the body may be in state of rest or motion.

## Example of inertia of motion.

Applying brake suddenly when the car is in motion. This explains as follows:

When the car is moving in a straight line at constant speed. And if we apply the brake, it goes slow down and Stop after some time. Due to the inertia of motion. Because the moving car always wants to remains in motion as according to Newton's first law. But when we apply brake, Newton's law break. That's the reason we feel forward force after applying brake.

Now, the question is which has more inertia.

1. An empty box.

2. A box with full of books.

Hence, to answer this question. Let's first understand that the object which has more masses has more inertia than the lighter one.

So, here the box full of books has more inertia than the empty box.

## *Daily life examples of inertia of motion with visual picture*

1. Feel backward force when car suddenly start.
2. Feel forward force when car suddenly stops.
3. Collision of moving objects in space.
4. Moving of satellite in space.

5. Moving of planets in space.
6. Jump from moving train.
7. Objects come to you when throw inside the moving train.
8. Athletes not stop running even after reach to the final position.
9. The moving of bike for some time, even we off the engine.
10. Continuous moving of stone attached with thread in circular path.

These are the 10 most common and familiar examples of inertia of motion that we have expressed in our life.

## *Application of inertia of motion*

- Application of car brakes, train brakes etc works on the inertia of motion.

- The runner athelete also uses the application of inertia of motion for long jumping.

- The scientist also uses the application of inertia of motion in space satellite.

- The study of the motion of earth and other planets can be understood by the application inertia of motion.

- Aeroplane take off and landing is also use application of inertia of motion.

## *Why inertia of motion related to Newton's first law*

According to Newton's first law of motion, a rest body always remains in state of rest and a moving object always in state of motion.

Hence, inertia of motion said that, a body which is moving with some velocity. It always moving forever until or unless an external force is applied to it.

So, the definition of both the term are inter relative. Not only the definition but also the concept of both the terms are co-related.

**Linear momentum**

It is measured by the products of the mass of the particle and its velocity. If m is the mass of the particle and V its linear Velocity then its momentum is P = mv

- Momentum is denoted by P.
- It is a Vector quantity.
- If the direction of momentum is same as that of Velocity.
- S.I unit of momentum P = mv.

## What is Linear momentum?

P = g cm/s.

S.I unit of momentum is kg m/s.

C.G.S unit of momentum is g cm/s.

**Case – I**

If m = constant then p $\alpha$ v. It means that if two different bodies have same mass then momentum will be greater for the body moving faster.

**Case-II**

If V = Constant. Then p $\alpha$ m.

It means that if the body have same speed the momentum will be greater for heavy bodies.

**In P = mv**

If M > m then PM > pm. It means that heavier one has greater momentum

**Case – III**

If two objects have equal momentum i.e. P = constant then

**Example :- Question :-**

1. *A body of mass 3kg is moving with a velocity of 2m /s in the east direction. What is the linear momentum of the body? What is its direction?*

P = mv.

P = 3× 2

P = 6kg m/s. towards east.

**Q.** *How much momentum will a dumb-bell of mass 10kg transfer to the floor if it falls from a height of 80 cm? Take its downward acceleration to be 10m /s².*

U = o, h = d = 80cm, Acceleration = g = 10 $m/s^2$

$V^2 = u^2 + 2as$,

$V^2 = 0^2 + 2\times 10\times 80100$

$V^2$ = o+20×80100

$V^2$=16

V=16

## Newton's Second law of Motion

According to Newton 2nd Law of motion the rate of change of momentum of a body is proportional to the external force acting on it and takes place in the direction of force.

According to Newton's 2nd law :-

Force α Change in rate of momentum. Or

F α Δ PΔ+

Or

F αΔ (m v )Δ+

Since the mass of the body remains Constant for small velocities and momentum is measured by the product of mass and velocity , the momentum can change only due to the change in velocity.

F α mΔ vΔ+

We know that rate of change of velocity with respect to time is known as acceleration.

Δ V Δ+ =a

Or, F $\alpha$ ma.

Or, F = Kma

Where K=Constant of proportionality.

If m=1, a=1, then F=1.

Put this value in equation

F = k×*1*×*1*

1 = k×*1*

From equation (i) and (ii)

F = ma

K = 1

## ***Meaning of arrow :-***

The direction of acceleration of a body is same as that of the force acting on it.

**Q.** *A body of mass 2kg is pulled by a constant force so that its acceleration is 1 $m/s^2$ towards north. Find the magnitude and direction of the force.*

*F= ma.*

F=2N,towards north

*F=2×1*

**Q.** *A hockey ball of mass 200g travelling at 10m/s is struck by a hockey stick so as to return it a long its original part with a velocity at 5m/s calculate change of momentum occurred in the motion of the hockey ball by the force applied by the hockey stick.*

*M= 2001000 kg,* u= 10m/s.

V= -5m/s.

Change in momentum= mv-mu.

m ( v-a )

*=2001000×(-5-10)*

*=15×-15*

= -3 kg m/s

**Q.** *An object of mass 100kg is accelerated uniformly from a velocity of 5m/s to 8m/s in 6 second. Calculate the initial and final momentum of the object, also find the magnitude of the force exerted on the object.*

*Mass of the object = 100kg,*

U = 5m/s, V = 8m/s, T = 6 sec.

Acceleration = (V-Ut)

= (8-56)

= *36*

= *0.5m/s*$^2$

*Force = ma*

*F = 100 ×0.510*

*F = 50N*

*Rate of change of momentum = mv – mu = m(v-u)*

*Initial momentum = mu*

= *100 × 5*

= *500m/s*

*Final momentum = mv.*

= *100 × 8*

= *800m/s*

**Q.** *Two objects each of mass 1.5kg are moving in the same straight line but in opposite direction. The velocity of each object is 2.5 m/s before the collision during which they stick together, what will be the velocity of the combined object after the collision.*

$m_1u_1 + m_2u_2 = m_1v_1 + m_2v_2$

*1.5×2.5+1.5×-2.5=v1.5+1.5*

*1.5×2.5-1.5×2.5=v 3.0*

*0 = 3v*

*V = 0m/s.*

**Unit of Force**

The force is expressed eighter in absolute or in gravitational units.

**Absolute unit of Forces:-**

An absolute unit of force which produces in a unit mass for a unit acceleration.

The absolute unit of force is in CGS system and SI system are dyne and Newton. (Expressed by the symbols dyne and N).

Dyne and Newton both the words are well known to us. We all study about that in class 9. But If we have remembered that there would be a relation exist between Dyne and Newton. So before we start discussing about relation. we should have recall both the terms Dyne and Newton in detail. After that we not only established the relation between Newton and Dyne but also derive the relation.

**What is Newton?**

Newton is the S.I unit of force. Which is denoted by N. Apart from this concept. Newton was a scientist. He discovered gravitation, and also very famous three laws of motion. He also write some novel on optics, calculus etc.

One Newton is defined as: A body of mass 1 kg travelling with the acceleration of 1m/s2. means 1 N = 1kg ✖ 1m/s2.

F = ma

Newton = kg . m/s2.

**What is Dyne?**

It is the C.G.S unit of force. It is denoted by "Dyne". If we define one dyne then it is a body of one gram of mass travelling with the acceleration of one centimeter per second square. i.e, 1 Dyne = 1g ✖ 1cm/s2.

F = ma

Dyne = 1g . cm/s2

**Relation between Dyne and Newton**

The mathematical relation between Newton and Dyne is, one newton is equal to the ten to the power five dyne. i.e,

1 Newton = 10^5 Dyne

In other words, the main relation between newton and dyne is both the term has same property. Means both have a unit of Force. But the difference is one have S.I unit and other is C.G.S unit.

- S.I unit of force is Newton
- C.G.S unit of force is Dyne.

**Derivation of relation between Newton and Dyne**

Here below are the derivation of relation between Dyne and Newton.

As we know that Force is the product of mass and acceleration. That means in mathematical terms F = ma. we also studied that force is the cross product of mass and acceleration.

F = ma

Force = mass x acceleration

Force = kg x m/s2 --------------- (1)

Now, change it in C.G.S unit. then,

Force = 1000 gram x 100 cm/s2 ------------ (2)

From equ. 1 and 2 we get,

1 kg x 1 m/s2 = 1000 gram x 100 cm/s2

1 Newton (from the definition of one newton) = 1000 x 100 x 1 gram . 1cm/s2

1 Newton = 10^5 x 1 gram . 1 cm/s2

1 Newton = 10^5 x 1 Dyne (from the definition of 1 Dyne)

1 Newton = 10^5 Dyne

Hence, the relation between Dyne and Newton is 1 Newton = 10^5 Dyne.

## Gravitational or Practical Unit of Force

A gravitational unit of force is defined as the force with which a body of unit mass is attracted by the earths towards its center.

The gravitational unit of force in CGS system and SI unit are gram Force and kilogram Force (also called gram weight) and Kilogram weight respectively.

## Newton's First laws of motion is contained in the second law of motion

According to the Newton first law of motion the position of object does not change if external force is not applied.

So if no external force is acting on the body then,

F = 0 N

Now, According to $2^{nd}$ law of motion

F = ma

a = $Fm$

a = $0m$

a = 0

= $v_2 - v_1 t2\text{-}t1$ = 0

$= v_2 - v_1 = 0$

$V_2 = v_1$

It means that if no external force is applied on a moving object then its initial and final velocities are equal. i.e, there is no change in the state of motion or velocity.

Hence, we can say that first law of motion is contained in the second law of motion.

**What is Impulse?**

Or Change In Momentum :- The Impulse of a force acting on a body is equal to the product of the force and the time for which it acts on a body.

A Force which acts upon a body for a very short time is called an impulsive force.

Impulse as the product of force and the time for which the force acts and its is equal to the total change in momentum.

It is denoted by I.

$I = F \times t$

Impulse is a vector quantity. Its direction is same as that of change in momentum of force.

Impulse = Change in momentum

$F \times t = mv - mu$

$F \times t = m(v\text{-}u)$

**Application of Impulse**

While catching a fast moving cricket ball, the players lower his hands along with the ball.

A person falling from a certain height, receive more several injuries if he falls on a cemental floor while, if he falls on a heap of sand or cotton, he had no injuries.

One more examples to illistrate our confusion on impulse. Lets suppose an athelet after finishing a race, runs for a while and stops. He does not stop in its final potision where race ends. He takes some more distance, due to the momentum of his body called impulse or impulsive force.

**Newton's Third law of Motion**

According to Newton's third law of motion for every action there is an equal and opposite reaction.

Action and reaction do not cancel each other because they acts on different bodies.

Force always occur in pair.

$N = mg$

Action and reaction acts simultanously out of the pair of forces only force can be called action and the other reaction.

**Examples of Newton's third law**

During acceleration of a car the tyre pushes on road and road also pushes back the tyre.

Second example, A rocket pushes on the exhaust gas and it turn the exhaust gas pushes back to the rocket so that rocket moves.

**Laws of conservation of momentum**

According to the laws of conservation of momentum total initial momentum is equal to final momentum.

$m_1u_1 + m_2u_2 = m_1v_1 + m_2v_2$

**Application :-**

- Recol of Gun
- Suddenly start the car at high speed in plane ground.

-------- ***Team Science laws*** ---------

# 4

# Sound and its laws

## *What is sound?*

- sound is a form of energy.
- All vibrating body produced sound.
- sound is that form of energy which makes us here.

## *Characteristic of sound*

Sound needs a material medium to travels.

**Medium:**- The substance through which sound travels is called a medium.

Note:- Hence we can say sound can travels through a medium solid, liquid and gasses, but it cannot travels through vaccum.

## ***Sound can travels through solid***

If a child speaks into one tin he can be here by another child who puts his ear to the other tin. It means that sound can travels through solid.

## ***Sound can travels through liquid***

If we fill a balloon with water and hold it near our ear then hit by a finger in lower side of the balloon with some force then we observe that some is hearing, so we conclude by this experiment when we git balloon then water molecules vibrate up and down rapidly and we here sound.

it means that sound can travels through water.

## ***Sound can travels through gasses***

When our parents talk to each other then we here sound because of disturbance of the particles of the air. we know that air is a gas so, sound can travels through gas.

it is the same reason for telephone bell when it ring.

## ***Sound can't travels through vaccum***

- A material medium ( like air ) is necessary for propagation of sound.

  The case of moon and the outer space this happens as follows:-

- In outer space there is no air present so we know that for propagation of sound a material medium must be able to carry sound waves from one place to another place but there is no material medium is present so sound cannot travels through vaccum. also sound cannot be hered in outer space or even in any place where air is not present then sound cannot travels on there. for propagation of sound there is very - very necessary a material medium like air.

- We cannot be talked on the moon like on the earth so space man can talk by radio wave. radio wave can travels through vaccum or in empty space because it an electromagnetic wave. we discuss about electromagnetic waves in latter topic.

## ***Sound travels in the form of waves***

sound travels in the form of wave or even light also travels in the form of waves. we all know that sound is a form of energy so wave carry energy. wave is a vibrating disturbance in the air which carry energy from one place to another place.

Sound is a disturbance in the the medium and it is also a form of energy so sound wave carry energy from one point to another point.

If we through a stone into a pond then we saw a concentric circle in the pond produced that is called the wave of sound namely transverse wave.

when a water waves passes over the surface of the water in a pond, there is no actual movement of water from the center to the side of the pond only the water molecules vibrates up and down about their fixed positions due to this reason water molecules appears to be moving to us.

- A periodic disturbance produce in a material medium due to the vibrating motion of the particles of medium is called wave.

## ***Wave motion:-***

It is the movement of disturbance produce to in one part of a medium to another involving the transfer of energy but not the transfer of matter, is called wave motion.

example:- Formation of ripples on the water surface. and propagation of sound wave through air or any other material medium.

## ***Characteristic of wave motion***

1. In wave motion the particles of the medium vibrate about their mean position. the particls of the medium do not move from one place to another place.
2. A wave motion travels by the same speed in all direction from the sound producing object in any medium.
3. In wave motion medium do not moves but the disturbance travels through the medium.
4. During a wave motion energy is transfer from one point of the medium to the another there is no transfer of matter through the medium.

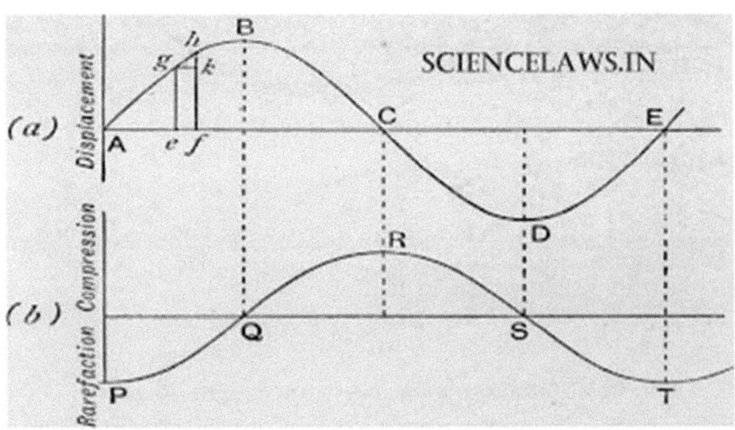


Enter Caption

## ***Mechanical wave and Non mechanical wave***

**Mechanical wave:-**

- The wave which need a material medium for their propagation are called mechanical wave.
- The medium may be solid, liquid or gas.
- Mechanical wave propagate through a medium due to the elastic properties of the medium due to this reason mechanical wave are also called elastic wave.
- Mechanical waves cannot travels through vaccum.
- Mechanical waves may be longitudinal, transverse wave.
- Speed of mechanical waves are low and depends upon the source and the medium through which they travels.
- Mechanical waves are due to the vibrations of the particles of the medium.
- Example of mechanical waves are sound waves and water waves.

**Non mechanical wave:-**

- The wave which do not need any material medium for their propagation of the sound is called non mechanical wave.
- Non mechanical wave can also travels through a material medium as well as vaccum.
- Electromagnetic waves are also called non mechanical waves.
- Light waves are non mechanical waves.
- Non mechanical wave can travels through vaccum.

**Electromagnetic wave :-**

- The wave which are associated with oscillating electrical and magnetic field and which do not need any material medium for the propagation of sound are called electromagnetic wave.
- electromagnetic wave can even travels through vaccum. ex. light waves, redio waves, television wave and x ray are electromagnetic waves.
- Electromagnetic waves are transverse wave.
- Electromagnetic waves travels with a speed of 3 x 10^8 m/s.
- The speed of an electromagnetic waves in any material medium is less then that in vaccum.
- Sound waves travels with low speed about 344 m/s at 20° C in air.
- Light wave and radio wave travels with velocity of light.

## ***Longitudinal wave and Transverse wave***

**Longitudinal wave:-**

- In this wave particles of the medium vibrate to and fro about their mean position in the direction of propagation of the wave is called a longitudinal wave.

SCIENCELAWS.IN

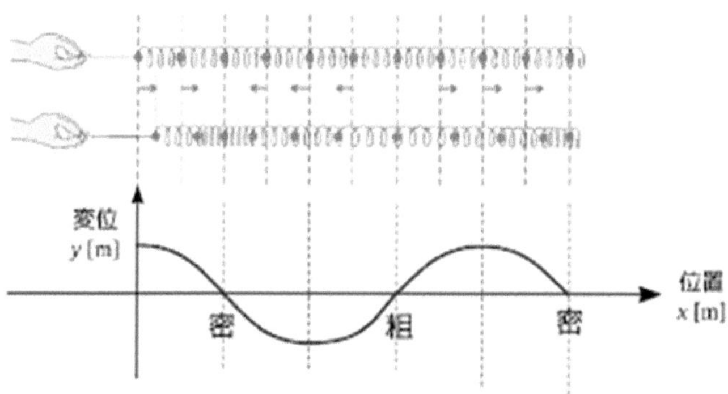


Enter Caption

- The wave which travels along a spring when it is pushed and pulled at one end are called longitudinal wave.
- Longitudinal wave can be produced in any medium ( like solid, liquid or gas ) . ex:- when a sound wave passes through air the particles of air vibrate back and forth parallel to the direction of sound wave.
- When the vibrating particles come closer to one another then their is a movementry reduction in volume and a compression is formed, on the other hand when the vibrating particles apart from one another then they normally their is a movementry increases in volume and a rarefaction is formed.

Experiment to show that how compression and rarefaction is formed in air.

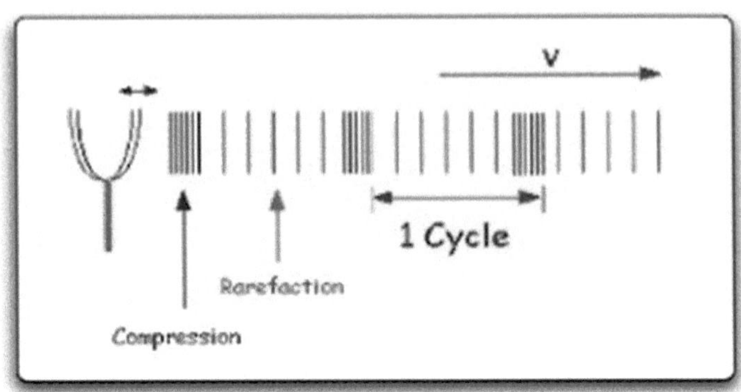


Enter Caption

## *Compression:-*

It is the part of a longitudinal wave in which the particles of the medium are closer to one another.

## *Rarefaction:-*

It is the part of a longitudinal wave in which the particles of the medium are further apart from the normal is called rarefaction.

## *Transverse wave:-*

A wave in which the particles of the medium vibrate up and down at right angle to the direction in which the wave is moving is called a transverse wave.

- Transverse wave can be produced only in solid and liquid but not in gas.
- Example:- when a stone is droped in a pond of water, transverse water waves are produced on the surface of water. even the light wave and radio waves are transverse wave because this wave cannot travels through air we know that transverse wave also cannot consist of medium gases.
- A transverse wave travels horizontally in a medium, the particles of the medium vibrate up and down in the vertical direction.
- The wave propagates in the form of crest and trough.
- These waves can travels through solid and on the surface of liquid only, as the propagation of these waves causes change in the shape of the medium.
- As there is no vibration of volume, there is no vibration in the density of the medium while the wave propagates through it.
- There is no created in pressure in the medium while the wave propagate.

## ***Transverse wave described Graphically***

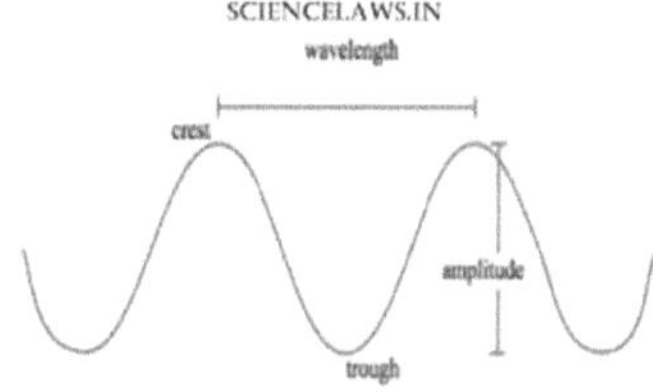


Enter Caption

**Crest;-**

The point of maximum position displacement on a transverse wave is called a crest.

**Trough;-**

The point of maximum negative depth displacement on a transverse wave is called trough.

## characteristics of sound waves

**characteristic of a sound wave**:- A sound wave can be described by five characteristic these are

1. Wavelength
2. Amplitude
3. Time period
4. Frequency
5. Velocity

## *Wavelength:-*

- The distance between the two nearest crest of a wave is called its wavelength.
- The minimum distance in which a sound wave repeats itself is called its wavelength.
- In other words it is the length of one complete wave.
- The distance between neighboring crest and trough is equal to half of the wavelength.
- Wavelength is denoted by lambda ( $\lambda$ ).
- S.I unit of wavelength is 'm' .

## ***Amplitude:-***

- The height of the crest or the depth of the trough of a wave is called amplitude.
- It is denoted by 'A'.
- Its S.I unit is 'm' .
- The amplitude of a wave is a measure of its energy hence the greater of the amplitude of a wave the greater is the energy.

## ***Frequency:-***

- The number of wave produced per second is called frequency.
- Frequency is denoted by ? or read as (nu) or f.
- The unit of frequency is Hz.
- example:- If 30 waves cycle are produced in one second then the frequency of the periodic wave is 30 Hz or 30 cycle/s.
- Note:- Frequency of a wave does not depend upon the nature of the medium through which it is travels hence the frequency of the wave remains the same as like solid, liquid and gas.

## ***Time period:-***

- The time required to produce on complete wave is called the time period of the wave.
- The S.I unit of time period is second 's' .
- It is denoted by letter 'T'.

## ***Wave velocity:-***

- The distance traveled by wave in one second is called wave velocity.
- It is denoted by letter 'V'.
- The S.I unit of wave velocity is m/s.
- The velocity of the wave depends upon the material medium through which they travels.
- speed of sound in air 343 m/s at 20 degree C.
- Speed of sound depend on medium as I say in the previous line.

## ***Relation between Time period and its frequency***

We know that time required to complete one wave is called time period.

Number of wave produce in 'T' sec. = 1

Number of wave produce in 1 sec. = 1/T

but,

we know that No. of wave produce in one second is called frequency,

∴ Frequency = 1/ time period

F = 1/ T

Relation between wave velocity, Frequency and wavelength for a periodic wave.

velocity of wave = wavelength x Frequency

## *Sonic Boom:-*

When a body moves with a velocity which is greater than the speed of sound in air then it is said to be travelling at supersonic speed. ( such as jet fighter plane or bullet gun ), and when they produce a sharp loud sound called a sonic boom.

## ***Sound depends on many things.***

1. Pitch
2. Loudness
3. Quality of musical sound

## ***Pitch:-***

We can distinguish between a man's voice and a women's voice of the same loudness even without seeing them. this is because a man's voice and a women's voice differ in pitch.

A man's voice is flat having a low pitch, whereas a women's voice is shrill having a high pitch.

- Pitch is that characteristic of sound by which we can distinguished between different sound of the same loudness.
- Pitch of the sound depends upon the frequency of the vibration.
- Pitch of the sound is directly proportional to its frequency.

## ***loudness:-***

- The loudness of sound is a measure of the sound energy reaching the ear per second.
- Loudness of the sound depends on the amplitude of sound wave.
- The greater the amplitude of sound wave , louder the sound will be.
- The S.I unit of loudness of sound is decibel. ' dB '.
- The softest sound which human ears can here is said to have a loudness of zero decibel.
- The loudness of sound of people talking quietly is about 65 decibel.

## ***Reflection of sound***

- The bouncing back of sound when it strikes on a hard surface is called reflection of sound.
- Sound waves are much longer than light wave so they required a much large area for reflection.

9 798887 174174

Printed by Libri Plureos GmbH in Hamburg,
Germany